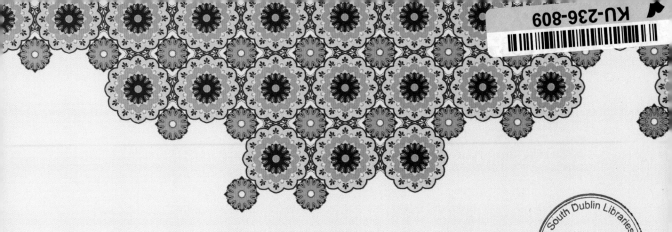

Religions Around the World

Buddhism

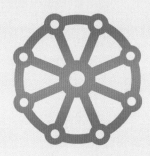

Anita Ganeri

raintree

a Capstone company — publishers for children

Raintree is an imprint of Capstone Global Library Limited, a company incorporated in England and Wales having its registered office at 264 Banbury Road, Oxford, OX2 7DY – Registered company number: 6695582

www.raintree.co.uk
myorders@raintree.co.uk

Edited by Linda Staniford
Designed by Jenny Bergstrom
Picture research by Pam Mitsakos
Production by Steve Walker
Originated by Capstone Global Library
Printed and bound in India

ISBN 978 1 4747 4218 4 (hardback)
21 20 19 18 17
10 9 8 7 6 5 4 3 2 1

ISBN 978 1 474 74224 5 (paperback)
22 21 20 19 18
10 9 8 7 6 5 4 3 2 1

British Library Cataloguing in Publication Data
A full catalogue record for this book is available from the British Library.

Acknowledgements
We would like to thank the following for permission to reproduce photographs: Alamy: FineArt, 24; Newscom: Alexandra Radu/Sipa USA, 26, Design Pics/Keith Levit, 18, DIEGO AZUBEL/EPA, 20, SAWAGUCHI/EPA, 28, Simon Montgomery/robertharding, 10; Shutterstock: 88studio, 15, Alexander Mazurkevich, 5, 25, AVA Bitter, cover middle, 1 middle, Chokchai Suksatavonraphan, 7, Kitti Tantibankul, 23, Liudmyla Matviiets, design element, Monkey Business Images, 12, Nila Newsom, 16, Ninja SS, 17, nuttavut sammongkol, 22, OlegD, 27, Pierre Jean Durieu, 6, R.M. Nunes, 4, SARIN KUNTHONG, 14, Stephane Bidouze, 13, Stephen Bures, 19, Suriya99, 11, Vasin Lee, 8, Visun Khankasem, 21; SuperStock: Steve Vidler, 9; Wikimedia: Pixabay, 29

We would like to thank Reverend Laurence Hillel of the London Inter Faith Centre for his invaluable help in the preparation of this book.

Every effort has been made to contact copyright holders of material reproduced in this book. Any omissions will be rectified in subsequent printings if notice is given to the publisher.

Contents

Some words are shown in bold, **like this.** You can find out what they mean by looking in the glossary.

What is Buddhism?

Buddhism is a religion that began in India more than 2,500 years ago. From India it spread across Asia. Today, around 500 million people follow Buddhism.

Buddhist monks sit under the bodhi tree at Bodhi Gaya in India, where the Buddha gained **enlightenment**.

This **image** of the Buddha is in a temple in Thailand.

People who follow Buddhism are called
Buddhists. Buddhists live all over the world.
China is the country with the most Buddhists.
Around 175,000 Buddhists live in Britain.

Buddhist beliefs

Buddhists do not believe that there is a God. They follow the teachings of a man named Siddhartha Gautama. He is called the Buddha. This means **"enlightened** one".

This **image** of the Buddha is in Nepal.

This is Lumbini, Nepal, where the Buddha was born.

Siddhartha was a royal prince. He lived in a palace and led an easy life. But when he left the palace, he saw that many people were unhappy. Only a **holy** man he met seemed to be content.

Siddhartha wanted to find out why the people were unhappy. One day he sat down under a tree to **meditate.** There he gained **enlightenment.** He understood why many people are unhappy.

The lotus flower floats on the water. Buddhists believe this is a symbol of rising above unhappiness.

The first people the Buddha taught were five **holy** men.

From then on, he was called the Buddha. He taught that people suffer because they are greedy. They are never happy with what they have got. They always want something more.

The eight spokes on this wheel stand for the eight steps on the path to happiness.

The Buddha taught people that there is a way to make their lives better. He showed them a path to follow so that they could find happiness. The path showed eight ways that people should live. One way was to be kind and caring towards other people. Another way was to do a job that does good in the world.

The Buddha also said that people should act and think in a calm way. They should train their minds to be calm and peaceful by **meditating** (see pages 16–17).

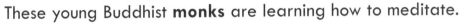

These young Buddhist **monks** are learning how to meditate.

Buddhist worship

Buddhists worship at home or in a **vihara**. They can worship on their own or with others. Worship is a way of paying **respect** and saying "thank you" to the Buddha.

At home, Buddhists pray in front of an image of the Buddha which they keep in a shrine.

This girl is offering a gift of lotus flowers in a vihara in Vietnam.

Buddhists worship in front of an **image** of the Buddha. They bow and put their hands together to show respect. They offer gifts of flowers, candles and **incense**.

For Buddhists, the Buddha and his teachings are like precious jewels. As part of worship, Buddhists **recite** some **verses**. The verses show how important the Buddha's teachings are to them.

Young Buddhist **monks** learn about the Buddha's teachings from older monks.

Buddhists are **vegetarians**. One of their rules is not to kill or harm animals.

Buddhists also promise to follow five rules in their lives. The most important is not killing or harming living things. This means being kind and caring at all times.

These **monks** are meditating in a monastery in India.

Buddhists try to **meditate** every day.
They sit cross-legged on the floor and
close their eyes. Then they breathe in
and out slowly. This helps them to feel
calm and quiet.

Most people like to sit cross-legged to meditate.

Buddhists believe that meditating helps them to slow down and see life more clearly. It helps them to think about the things that are really important.

Monks and nuns

Some Buddhists become **monks** and **nuns**. They spend their lives **meditating** and reading the **sacred** texts. They help ordinary people to understand the Buddha's teachings.

This monk is reading the sacred texts in a monastery in China.

These young boys are Buddhist monks in Burma.

In some countries, boys become monks for just a few years. They live in a **vihara** with the other monks. Like the monks, they have their heads shaved and wear **robes**.

These monks wait to receive gifts at a **vihara**.

Monks and **nuns** must give up their personal belongings. They are only allowed to own eight things. These are three robes, a bowl, a razor, a needle, a belt and a **water filter**.

Buddhists living nearby give the monks and nuns gifts of food. They sometimes give them money. Giving things to the monks and nuns is part of a Buddhist's **duty**.

Monks receive gifts of food and other items from local Buddhist people.

Sacred texts

There are many **sacred** texts in Buddhism. The Tripitaka is a collection of stories, teachings and talks by the Buddha. It also includes rules for how **monks** and **nuns** should live.

The Tripitaka was first written down on rectangular palm leaves.

This picture is a scene from the Jatakas, which tell the story of the Buddha's life.

The Jatakas are part of the Tripitaka. They are more than 500 stories about the Buddha. The stories teach Buddhists about being kind, **generous** and caring to other people.

Another **sacred** text is the Lotus Sutra. It is a long talk that the Buddha gave. In it the Buddha says that he is like a rain cloud. He rains down his teaching on the world.

This is a page from the Lotus Sutra, written in Japanese.

These prayer stones in Tibet have mantras written on them.

In Tibet people write sacred words on stones and flags. These words are called **mantras.** People say the words over and over again to clear their minds for **meditation.**

Special days

There are many special days in the year for Buddhists. Many celebrate the Buddha's birthday and other times in his life. They take place at the time of the nearest full moon.

Candles are lit to celebrate the Buddha's birthday.

Children dress up in colourful costumes to celebrate Wesak in Sri Lanka.

Wesak is the most important Buddhist festival. It falls in April or May and is held to celebrate the Buddha's life. People light lamps and candles. Their light is like the Buddha's teaching.

These children are celebrating Hana Matsuri, which is also called the Flower Fesitval.

In April, Buddhists in Japan celebrate the festival of Hana Matsuri. This remembers the Buddha's birthday. Legend says that he was born in a beautiful garden filled with flowers.

Sangha Day is a Buddhist festival marked in Britain in November. It is held to celebrate the community of Buddhists, which is called the sangha. It is a day for friendship and being together.

On Sangha Day, people meet together to make their Buddhist faith stronger.

Glossary

duty something a person must or ought to do

enlightenment wisdom, truth or understanding

generous willing to give and share with others

holy sacred, devoted to religion

image statue or picture of someone or something

incense substance burned to produce a pleasant smell

mantra sacred word or phrase, often chanted as a prayer

meditate think deeply and quietly as a way of relaxing your mind and body

monk man who lives in a religious community and devotes his life to his religion

nun woman who lives in a religious community and devotes her life to her religion

recite say aloud something that has been memorized

respect feeling of admiration or high regard

robe loose garment worn for ceremonies

sacred holy, deserving great respect

sangha community of Buddhist monks and nuns

vegetarian a person who does not eat meat

verse section of a poem or song

vihara Buddhist monastery or temple

water filter device that cleans water as it passes through it

Find out more

Books

Buddhism (Our Places of Worship), Honor Head
(Wayland, 2009)

Celebrating Buddhist Festivals (Celebration Days), Nick Hunter
(Raintree, 2015)

We are Buddhists (My Religion and Me), Philip Blake
(Franklin Watts, 2015)

Websites

www.bbc.co.uk/schools/religion/buddhist/
Find out more about Buddhism with this fact-packed website.

www.primaryhomeworkhelp.co.uk/religion/buddhism.htm
Discover lots of information about Buddhism to help you with
homework projects.

Index